Our Table Our Legacy

Where Every Recipe Tells a Story

Atosha Logan

Our Table Our Legacy

Where Every Recipe Tells a Story

Atosha Logan

FOR PERMISSION REQUESTS, CONTACT THE AUTHOR AT:
ATOSHA LOGAN, AUTHOR & PUBLISHER
INFO@ATOSHALOGAN.COM
WWW.ATOSHALOGAN.COM

ISBN:979-8-9931753-3-1 (PAPERBACK)

PRINTED IN THE UNITED STATES OF AMERICA

COVER DESIGN: ATOSHA LOGAN
INTERIOR LAYOUT: ATOSHA LOGAN

This book
belongs to:

_____

_____

BOOK DEDICATION

To my parents, Jerald & Willie Mae—
You were the first to place a spoon in my hand and the ones who taught me that every recipe carries more than flavor; it carries love, memory, and legacy. The lessons you passed down in the kitchen shaped not only my skills, but also my heart. Your hands seasoned the food, but your love seasoned my life.

This book exists because of you—your patience, your wisdom, and your unwavering love.

Our Table Our Legacy is a tribute to the meals we shared, the stories we told, and the love you entrusted to me. May your legacy continue to season every dish and inspire every generation that gathers at our table.
Love,
Your daughter,
Atosha

Introduction

At every table, a story is told.
Our family recipes are more than instructions for meals—they are a living testimony of love, laughter, resilience, and legacy.
Each dish carries the fingerprints of those who came before us, who stirred with care, seasoned with wisdom, and served with joy.
From holiday feasts to quiet suppers, the recipes within these pages remind us that food is more than sustenance; it is the thread that binds generations together.

This book is not just a collection of ingredients and steps—it is a keepsake, a treasure chest of memories meant to be preserved, shared, and passed down.
May every page inspire you to recreate flavors that echo the past, to celebrate traditions, and to create new memories at your own table.
Because when we gather, when we share a meal, and when we tell our stories, our legacy continues.

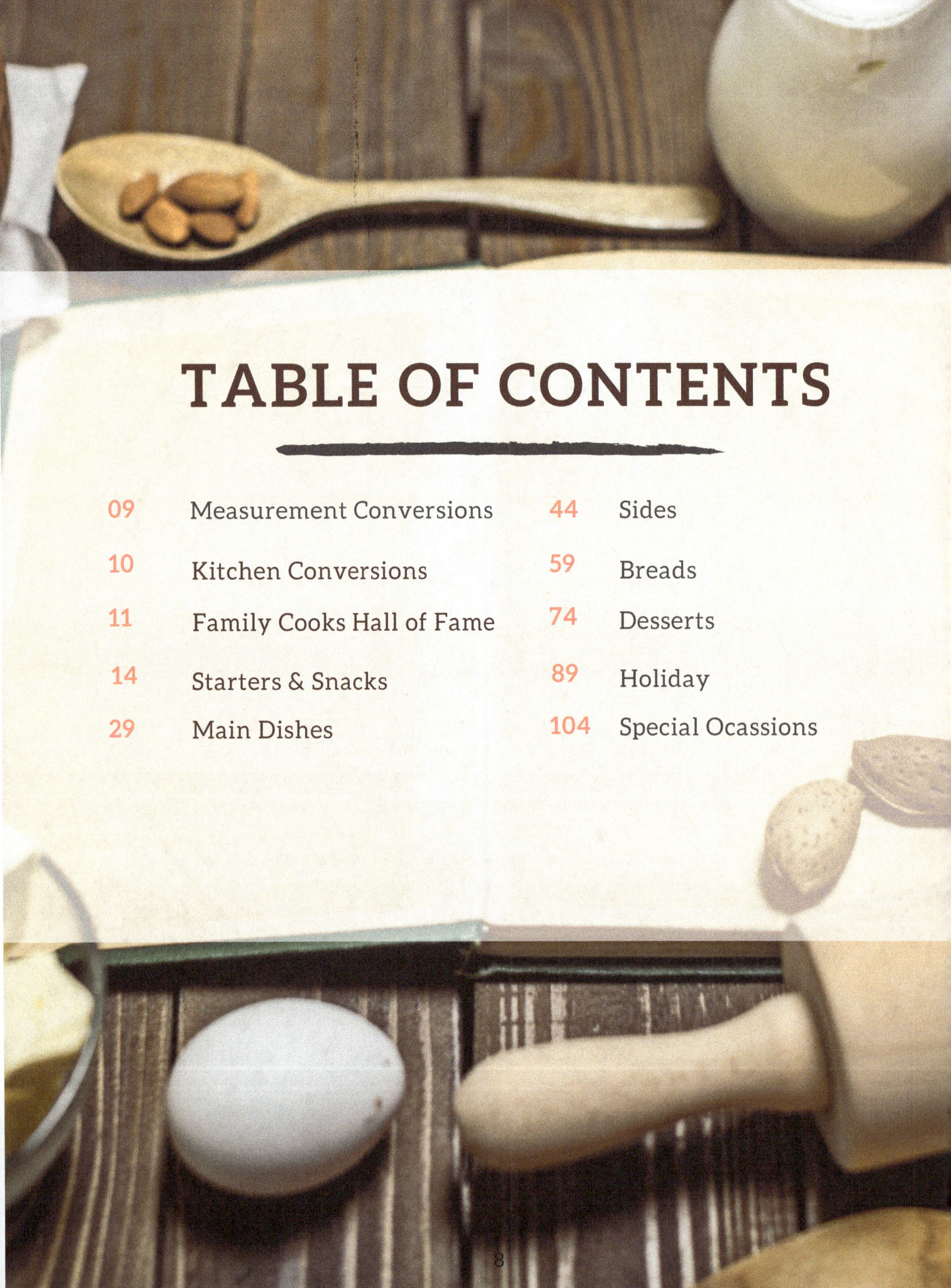

TABLE OF CONTENTS

MEASUREMENT CONVERSIONS

LENGTH

Customary Units

1 Foot = 12 Inches

1 Yard = 3 Feet

1 Mile = 5,280 Feet

Metric Units

1 Kilometer = 1,000 Meters

1 Meter = 100 centimeters

1 centimeter = 10 millimeters

CAPACITY

Customary Units

1 Gallon = 4 Quarts

1 Quart = 2 Pints

1 Pint = 2 Cups

1 Cup = 8 Fluid Ounces

Metric Units

1 liter = 10 Deciliters

1 liter = 1000 Millimeters

WEIGHT

Customary Units

1 Pound = 16 Ounces

1 Ton = 2,000 pounds

MASS

Metric Units

1 Kilogram = 1,000 Grams

1 Gram = 1,000 Milligrams

TIME

1 Minute = 60 Seconds

1 Hour = 60 Minutes

1 Day = 24 Hours

1 Week = 7 Days

1 Year = 12 Months

1 Year = 52 Weeks

1 Year = 365 Days

1 Leap Year = 366

KITCHEN
Conversions

1 GALLON
4 QUARTZ
8 PINTS
16 CUPS
128 OZ

1 QUARTZ
2 PINTS
4 CUPS
32 OZ

1 PINT
2 CUPS
16 OZ

1 CUP
16 TBS
48 TSP
8 OZ

1/2 CUP
8 TBS
24 TSP
4 OZ

1/4 CUP
4 TBS
12 TSP
2 OZ

1 TBS
3 TSP
1/2 OZ

1 TBS
8 PINCHES

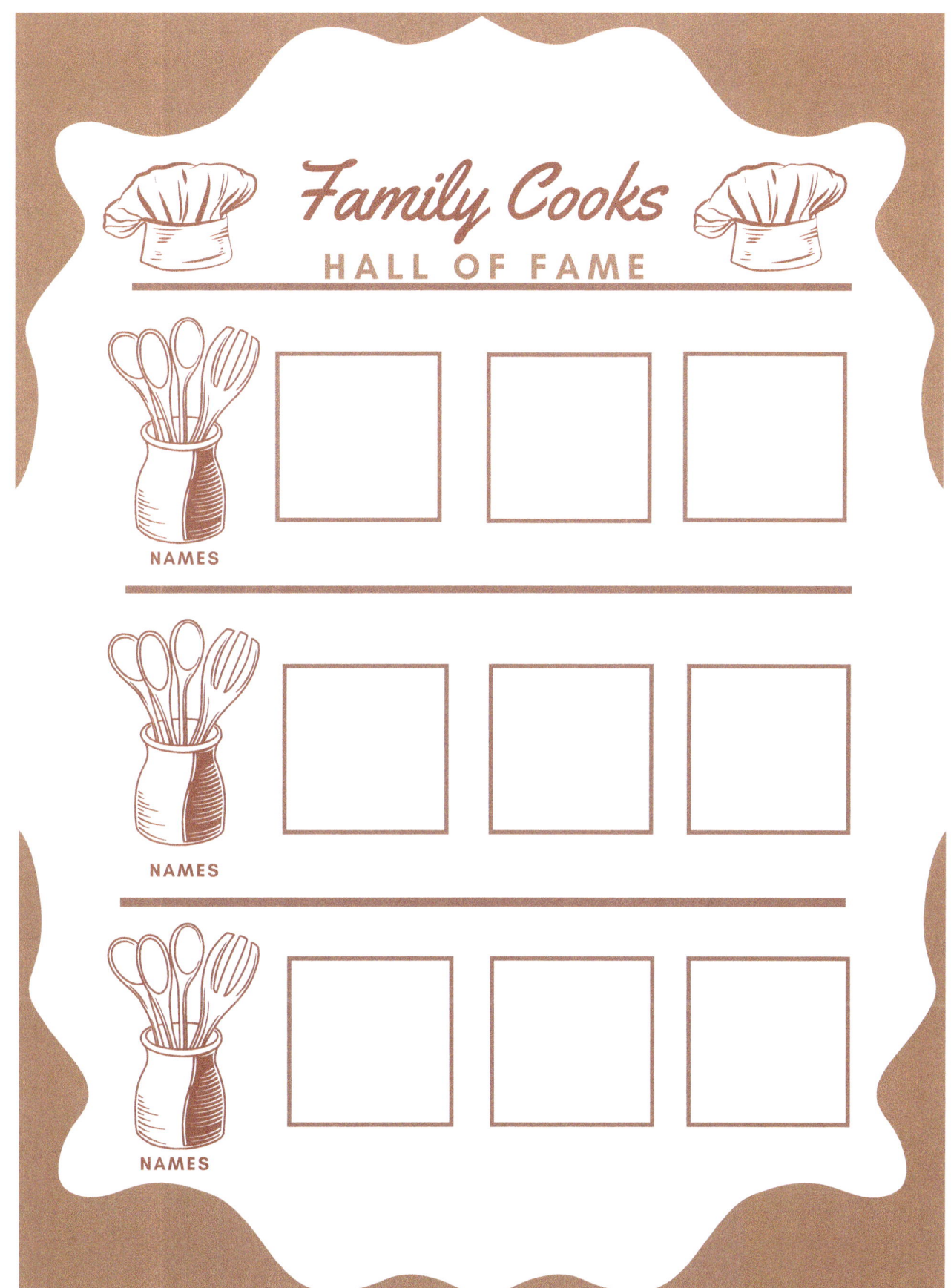

Family Cooks
HALL OF FAME

NAMES

NAMES

NAMES

.

Starters & Snacks

Let's *Cook*

First Bites

Lasting Memories

Our Table Our Legacy

NAME OF DISH

RECIPE OWNER

COOK TIME

SERVINGS

INGREDIENTS

-
-
-
-
-
-
-
-
-
-
-

DIRECTIONS

notes

☐ Vegetarian ☐ Vegan ☐ Dairy Free ☐ Gluten Free ☐ Low Carb

Our Table Our Legacy

NAME OF DISH

RECIPE OWNER

COOK TIME

SERVINGS

INGREDIENTS

-
-
-
-
-
-
-
-
-
-

DIRECTIONS

notes

☐ Vegetarian   ☐ Vegan   ☐ Dairy Free   ☐ Gluten Free   ☐ Low Carb

Our Table Our Legacy

NAME OF DISH

RECIPE OWNER

COOK TIME

SERVINGS

INGREDIENTS

-
-
-
-
-
-
-
-
-
-

DIRECTIONS

notes

☐ Vegetarian   ☐ Vegan   ☐ Dairy Free   ☐ Gluten Free   ☐ Low Carb

Our Table Our Legacy

NAME OF DISH

RECIPE OWNER

COOK TIME

SERVINGS

INGREDIENTS

-
-
-
-
-
-
-
-
-
-
-

DIRECTIONS

notes

☐ Vegetarian   ☐ Vegan   ☐ Dairy Free   ☐ Gluten Free   ☐ Low Carb

Our Table Our Legacy

NAME OF DISH

RECIPE OWNER

COOK TIME

SERVINGS

INGREDIENTS

- ....
- ....
- ....
- ....
- ....
- ....
- ....
- ....
- ....
- ....

DIRECTIONS

notes

☐ Vegetarian   ☐ Vegan   ☐ Dairy Free   ☐ Gluten Free   ☐ Low Carb

Our Table Our Legacy

NAME OF DISH

RECIPE OWNER

COOK TIME

SERVINGS

INGREDIENTS

- ....
- ....
- ....
- ....
- ....
- ....
- ....
- ....
- ....
- ....
- ....

DIRECTIONS

....
....
....
....
....
....
....
....
....
....
....
....
....
....
....

notes

☐ Vegetarian   ☐ Vegan   ☐ Dairy Free   ☐ Gluten Free   ☐ Low Carb

Our Table Our Legacy

NAME OF DISH

RECIPE OWNER	COOK TIME	SERVINGS

INGREDIENTS

-
-
-
-
-
-
-
-
-
-

DIRECTIONS

notes

☐ Vegetarian   ☐ Vegan   ☐ Dairy Free   ☐ Gluten Free   ☐ Low Carb

Our Table Our Legacy

NAME OF DISH

RECIPE OWNER   COOK TIME   SERVINGS

INGREDIENTS

- ....
- ....
- ....
- ....
- ....
- ....
- ....
- ....
- ....
- ....
- ....

DIRECTIONS

....
....
....
....
....
....
....
....
....
....
....
....
....
....
....
....

notes

☐ Vegetarian   ☐ Vegan   ☐ Dairy Free   ☐ Gluten Free   ☐ Low Carb

Our Table Our Legacy

NAME OF DISH

RECIPE OWNER

COOK TIME

SERVINGS

INGREDIENTS

- ....
- ....
- ....
- ....
- ....
- ....
- ....
- ....
- ....
- ....
- ....

DIRECTIONS

....
....
....
....
....
....
....
....
....
....
....
....
....
....

notes

☐ Vegetarian   ☐ Vegan   ☐ Dairy Free   ☐ Gluten Free   ☐ Low Carb

Our Table Our Legacy

NAME OF DISH

RECIPE OWNER

COOK TIME

SERVINGS

INGREDIENTS

- ....
- ....
- ....
- ....
- ....
- ....
- ....
- ....
- ....
- ....
- ....

DIRECTIONS

....
....
....
....
....
....
....
....
....
....
....
....
....

notes

☐ Vegetarian   ☐ Vegan   ☐ Dairy Free   ☐ Gluten Free   ☐ Low Carb

Main Dishes

Let's *Cook*

The Heart
of Our Table

Our Table Our Legacy

NAME OF DISH

RECIPE OWNER	COOK TIME	SERVINGS

INGREDIENTS

- ....
- ....
- ....
- ....
- ....
- ....
- ....
- ....
- ....
- ....
- ....

DIRECTIONS

notes

☐ Vegetarian   ☐ Vegan   ☐ Dairy Free   ☐ Gluten Free   ☐ Low Carb

Our Table Our Legacy

NAME OF DISH

RECIPE OWNER

COOK TIME

SERVINGS

INGREDIENTS

-
-
-
-
-
-
-
-
-
-

DIRECTIONS

notes

☐ Vegetarian ☐ Vegan ☐ Dairy Free ☐ Gluten Free ☐ Low Carb

Our Table Our Legacy

NAME OF DISH

RECIPE OWNER   COOK TIME   SERVINGS

INGREDIENTS

- ....
- ....
- ....
- ....
- ....
- ....
- ....
- ....
- ....
- ....

DIRECTIONS

notes

☐ Vegetarian   ☐ Vegan   ☐ Dairy Free   ☐ Gluten Free   ☐ Low Carb

34

Our Table Our Legacy

NAME OF DISH

RECIPE OWNER   COOK TIME   SERVINGS

INGREDIENTS

-
-
-
-
-
-
-
-
-
-
-

DIRECTIONS

notes

☐ Vegetarian   ☐ Vegan   ☐ Dairy Free   ☐ Gluten Free   ☐ Low Carb

Our Table Our Legacy

NAME OF DISH

RECIPE OWNER	COOK TIME	SERVINGS

INGREDIENTS

- ....
- ....
- ....
- ....
- ....
- ....
- ....
- ....
- ....
- ....
- ....

DIRECTIONS

....
....
....
....
....
....
....
....
....
....
....
....
....
....

notes

☐ Vegetarian　　☐ Vegan　　☐ Dairy Free　　☐ Gluten Free　　☐ Low Carb

Our Table Our Legacy

NAME OF DISH

RECIPE OWNER   **COOK TIME**   **SERVINGS**

INGREDIENTS

- ....
- ....
- ....
- ....
- ....
- ....
- ....
- ....
- ....
- ....

DIRECTIONS

....
....
....
....
....
....
....
....
....
....
....
....
....
....

notes

☐ Vegetarian   ☐ Vegan   ☐ Dairy Free   ☐ Gluten Free   ☐ Low Carb

Our Table Our Legacy

NAME OF DISH

RECIPE OWNER

COOK TIME

SERVINGS

INGREDIENTS

- ....
- ....
- ....
- ....
- ....
- ....
- ....
- ....
- ....
- ....

DIRECTIONS

....
....
....
....
....
....
....
....
....
....
....
....

notes

☐ Vegetarian   ☐ Vegan   ☐ Dairy Free   ☐ Gluten Free   ☐ Low Carb

Our Table Our Legacy

NAME OF DISH

RECIPE OWNER   COOK TIME   SERVINGS

INGREDIENTS

-
-
-
-
-
-
-
-
-
-
-

DIRECTIONS

notes

☐ Vegetarian   ☐ Vegan   ☐ Dairy Free   ☐ Gluten Free   ☐ Low Carb

Our Table Our Legacy

NAME OF DISH

RECIPE OWNER

COOK TIME

SERVINGS

INGREDIENTS

-
-
-
-
-
-
-
-
-
-
-

DIRECTIONS

notes

☐ Vegetarian ☐ Vegan ☐ Dairy Free ☐ Gluten Free ☐ Low Carb

Our Table Our Legacy

NAME OF DISH

RECIPE OWNER

COOK TIME

SERVINGS

INGREDIENTS

-
-
-
-
-
-
-
-
-
-

DIRECTIONS

notes

☐ Vegetarian　　☐ Vegan　　☐ Dairy Free　　☐ Gluten Free　　☐ Low Carb

DISH
PICTURE
COLLAGE

Sides

Let's *Cook*

Passed Around

with Love

Our Table Our Legacy

NAME OF DISH

RECIPE OWNER   COOK TIME   SERVINGS

INGREDIENTS

- ....
- ....
- ....
- ....
- ....
- ....
- ....
- ....
- ....
- ....
- ....

DIRECTIONS

....
....
....
....
....
....
....
....
....
....
....
....
....
....
....
....

notes

☐ Vegetarian   ☐ Vegan   ☐ Dairy Free   ☐ Gluten Free   ☐ Low Carb

Our Table Our Legacy

NAME OF DISH

RECIPE OWNER

COOK TIME

SERVINGS

INGREDIENTS

-
-
-
-
-
-
-
-
-
-
-

DIRECTIONS

notes

☐ Vegetarian   ☐ Vegan   ☐ Dairy Free   ☐ Gluten Free   ☐ Low Carb

Our Table Our Legacy

NAME OF DISH

RECIPE OWNER	COOK TIME	SERVINGS

INGREDIENTS

- ....
- ....
- ....
- ....
- ....
- ....
- ....
- ....
- ....
- ....

DIRECTIONS

....
....
....
....
....
....
....
....
....
....
....

notes

☐ Vegetarian ☐ Vegan ☐ Dairy Free ☐ Gluten Free ☐ Low Carb

Our Table Our Legacy

NAME OF DISH

RECIPE OWNER

COOK TIME

SERVINGS

INGREDIENTS

-
-
-
-
-
-
-
-
-
-

DIRECTIONS

notes

☐ Vegetarian ☐ Vegan ☐ Dairy Free ☐ Gluten Free ☐ Low Carb

Our Table Our Legacy

NAME OF DISH

RECIPE OWNER

COOK TIME

SERVINGS

INGREDIENTS

-
-
-
-
-
-
-
-
-
-

DIRECTIONS

notes

☐ Vegetarian   ☐ Vegan   ☐ Dairy Free   ☐ Gluten Free   ☐ Low Carb

Our Table Our Legacy

NAME OF DISH

RECIPE OWNER

COOK TIME

SERVINGS

INGREDIENTS

- ....
- ....
- ....
- ....
- ....
- ....
- ....
- ....
- ....
- ....

DIRECTIONS

....
....
....
....
....
....
....
....
....
....
....
....
....

notes

☐ Vegetarian ☐ Vegan ☐ Dairy Free ☐ Gluten Free ☐ Low Carb

Our Table Our Legacy

NAME OF DISH

RECIPE OWNER

COOK TIME

SERVINGS

INGREDIENTS

-
-
-
-
-
-
-
-
-
-

DIRECTIONS

notes

☐ Vegetarian   ☐ Vegan   ☐ Dairy Free   ☐ Gluten Free   ☐ Low Carb

Our Table Our Legacy

NAME OF DISH

RECIPE OWNER   COOK TIME   SERVINGS

INGREDIENTS

-
-
-
-
-
-
-
-
-
-

DIRECTIONS

notes

☐ Vegetarian   ☐ Vegan   ☐ Dairy Free   ☐ Gluten Free   ☐ Low Carb

Our Table Our Legacy

NAME OF DISH

RECIPE OWNER

COOK TIME

SERVINGS

INGREDIENTS

- ....
- ....
- ....
- ....
- ....
- ....
- ....
- ....
- ....
- ....
- ....

DIRECTIONS

notes

☐ Vegetarian ☐ Vegan ☐ Dairy Free ☐ Gluten Free ☐ Low Carb

Our Table Our Legacy

NAME OF DISH

RECIPE OWNER

COOK TIME

SERVINGS

INGREDIENTS

- ....
- ....
- ....
- ....
- ....
- ....
- ....
- ....
- ....
- ....

DIRECTIONS

....
....
....
....
....
....
....
....
....
....
....
....
....

notes

☐ Vegetarian   ☐ Vegan   ☐ Dairy Free   ☐ Gluten Free   ☐ Low Carb

Breads

Let's *Cook*

The Warmth

of Home

Our Table Our Legacy

NAME OF DISH

RECIPE OWNER

COOK TIME

SERVINGS

INGREDIENTS

-
-
-
-
-
-
-
-
-
-
-

DIRECTIONS

notes

☐ Vegetarian   ☐ Vegan   ☐ Dairy Free   ☐ Gluten Free   ☐ Low Carb

Our Table Our Legacy

NAME OF DISH

RECIPE OWNER

COOK TIME

SERVINGS

INGREDIENTS

-
-
-
-
-
-
-
-
-
-

DIRECTIONS

notes

☐ Vegetarian   ☐ Vegan   ☐ Dairy Free   ☐ Gluten Free   ☐ Low Carb

Our Table Our Legacy

NAME OF DISH

RECIPE OWNER

COOK TIME

SERVINGS

INGREDIENTS

- ....
- ....
- ....
- ....
- ....
- ....
- ....
- ....
- ....
- ....
- ....

DIRECTIONS

....
....
....
....
....
....
....
....
....
....
....
....
....
....

notes

☐ Vegetarian ☐ Vegan ☐ Dairy Free ☐ Gluten Free ☐ Low Carb

64

Our Table Our Legacy

NAME OF DISH

RECIPE OWNER   COOK TIME   SERVINGS

INGREDIENTS

- ....
- ....
- ....
- ....
- ....
- ....
- ....
- ....
- ....
- ....
- ....

DIRECTIONS

....
....
....
....
....
....
....
....
....
....
....
....
....
....

notes

☐ Vegetarian   ☐ Vegan   ☐ Dairy Free   ☐ Gluten Free   ☐ Low Carb

Our Table Our Legacy

NAME OF DISH

RECIPE OWNER

COOK TIME

SERVINGS

INGREDIENTS

- ....
- ....
- ....
- ....
- ....
- ....
- ....
- ....
- ....
- ....

DIRECTIONS

....
....
....
....
....
....
....
....
....
....
....
....
....
....

notes

☐ Vegetarian   ☐ Vegan   ☐ Dairy Free   ☐ Gluten Free   ☐ Low Carb

Our Table Our Legacy

NAME OF DISH

RECIPE OWNER

COOK TIME

SERVINGS

INGREDIENTS

-
-
-
-
-
-
-
-
-
-

DIRECTIONS

notes

☐ Vegetarian ☐ Vegan ☐ Dairy Free ☐ Gluten Free ☐ Low Carb

Our Table Our Legacy

NAME OF DISH

RECIPE OWNER   COOK TIME   SERVINGS

INGREDIENTS

- ....
- ....
- ....
- ....
- ....
- ....
- ....
- ....
- ....
- ....

DIRECTIONS

....
....
....
....
....
....
....
....
....
....
....
....
....
....

notes

☐ Vegetarian   ☐ Vegan   ☐ Dairy Free   ☐ Gluten Free   ☐ Low Carb

Our Table Our Legacy

NAME OF DISH

RECIPE OWNER

COOK TIME

SERVINGS

INGREDIENTS

- ....
- ....
- ....
- ....
- ....
- ....
- ....
- ....
- ....
- ....

DIRECTIONS

....
....
....
....
....
....
....
....
....
....
....
....
....

notes

☐ Vegetarian   ☐ Vegan   ☐ Dairy Free   ☐ Gluten Free   ☐ Low Carb

69

Our Table Our Legacy

NAME OF DISH

RECIPE OWNER

COOK TIME

SERVINGS

INGREDIENTS

-
-
-
-
-
-
-
-
-
-

DIRECTIONS

notes

☐ Vegetarian   ☐ Vegan   ☐ Dairy Free   ☐ Gluten Free   ☐ Low Carb

Our Table Our Legacy

NAME OF DISH

RECIPE OWNER   COOK TIME   SERVINGS

INGREDIENTS

-
-
-
-
-
-
-
-
-
-

DIRECTIONS

notes

☐ Vegetarian   ☐ Vegan   ☐ Dairy Free   ☐ Gluten Free   ☐ Low Carb

DISH
PICTURE
COLLAGE

Desserts

Let's *Cook*

Sweet Endings

Sweet Memories

Our Table Our Legacy

NAME OF DISH

RECIPE OWNER

COOK TIME

SERVINGS

INGREDIENTS

- ....
- ....
- ....
- ....
- ....
- ....
- ....
- ....
- ....
- ....
- ....

DIRECTIONS

notes

☐ Vegetarian   ☐ Vegan   ☐ Dairy Free   ☐ Gluten Free   ☐ Low Carb

Our Table Our Legacy

NAME OF DISH

RECIPE OWNER

COOK TIME

SERVINGS

INGREDIENTS

-
-
-
-
-
-
-
-
-
-
-

DIRECTIONS

notes

☐ Vegetarian   ☐ Vegan   ☐ Dairy Free   ☐ Gluten Free   ☐ Low Carb

Our Table Our Legacy

NAME OF DISH

RECIPE OWNER

COOK TIME

SERVINGS

INGREDIENTS

- ....
- ....
- ....
- ....
- ....
- ....
- ....
- ....
- ....
- ....
- ....

DIRECTIONS

notes

☐ Vegetarian   ☐ Vegan   ☐ Dairy Free   ☐ Gluten Free   ☐ Low Carb

Our Table Our Legacy

NAME OF DISH

RECIPE OWNER

COOK TIME

SERVINGS

INGREDIENTS

-
-
-
-
-
-
-
-
-
-
-

DIRECTIONS

notes

☐ Vegetarian   ☐ Vegan   ☐ Dairy Free   ☐ Gluten Free   ☐ Low Carb

Our Table Our Legacy

NAME OF DISH

RECIPE OWNER

COOK TIME

SERVINGS

INGREDIENTS

-
-
-
-
-
-
-
-
-
-

DIRECTIONS

notes

☐ Vegetarian   ☐ Vegan   ☐ Dairy Free   ☐ Gluten Free   ☐ Low Carb

Our Table Our Legacy

NAME OF DISH

RECIPE OWNER

COOK TIME

SERVINGS

INGREDIENTS

- ....
- ....
- ....
- ....
- ....
- ....
- ....
- ....
- ....
- ....

DIRECTIONS

notes

☐ Vegetarian   ☐ Vegan   ☐ Dairy Free   ☐ Gluten Free   ☐ Low Carb

Our Table Our Legacy

NAME OF DISH

RECIPE OWNER

COOK TIME

SERVINGS

INGREDIENTS

- ....
- ....
- ....
- ....
- ....
- ....
- ....
- ....
- ....
- ....
- ....

DIRECTIONS

....

....

....

....

....

....

....

....

....

....

....

....

notes

☐ Vegetarian   ☐ Vegan   ☐ Dairy Free   ☐ Gluten Free   ☐ Low Carb

Our Table Our Legacy

NAME OF DISH

RECIPE OWNER

COOK TIME

SERVINGS

INGREDIENTS

- ....
- ....
- ....
- ....
- ....
- ....
- ....
- ....
- ....
- ....
- ....

DIRECTIONS

notes

☐ Vegetarian   ☐ Vegan   ☐ Dairy Free   ☐ Gluten Free   ☐ Low Carb

Our Table Our Legacy

NAME OF DISH

RECIPE OWNER	COOK TIME	SERVINGS

INGREDIENTS

-
-
-
-
-
-
-
-
-
-

DIRECTIONS

notes

☐ Vegetarian ☐ Vegan ☐ Dairy Free ☐ Gluten Free ☐ Low Carb

Our Table Our Legacy

NAME OF DISH

RECIPE OWNER

COOK TIME

SERVINGS

INGREDIENTS

- ....
- ....
- ....
- ....
- ....
- ....
- ....
- ....
- ....
- ....
- ....

DIRECTIONS

notes

☐ Vegetarian ☐ Vegan ☐ Dairy Free ☐ Gluten Free ☐ Low Carb

DISH
PICTURE
COLLAGE

Holiday

Let's *Cook*

Recipes
that brought us together

Our Table Our Legacy

NAME OF DISH

RECIPE OWNER

COOK TIME

SERVINGS

INGREDIENTS

- ....
- ....
- ....
- ....
- ....
- ....
- ....
- ....
- ....
- ....

DIRECTIONS

....
....
....
....
....
....
....
....
....
....
....
....
....

notes

☐ Vegetarian   ☐ Vegan   ☐ Dairy Free   ☐ Gluten Free   ☐ Low Carb

Our Table Our Legacy

NAME OF DISH

RECIPE OWNER   COOK TIME   SERVINGS

INGREDIENTS

-
-
-
-
-
-
-
-
-
-

DIRECTIONS

notes

☐ Vegetarian   ☐ Vegan   ☐ Dairy Free   ☐ Gluten Free   ☐ Low Carb

Our Table Our Legacy

NAME OF DISH

RECIPE OWNER	COOK TIME	SERVINGS

INGREDIENTS

- ....
- ....
- ....
- ....
- ....
- ....
- ....
- ....
- ....
- ....

DIRECTIONS

notes

☐ Vegetarian ☐ Vegan ☐ Dairy Free ☐ Gluten Free ☐ Low Carb

Our Table Our Legacy

NAME OF DISH

RECIPE OWNER

COOK TIME

SERVINGS

INGREDIENTS

-
-
-
-
-
-
-
-
-
-

DIRECTIONS

notes

☐ Vegetarian ☐ Vegan ☐ Dairy Free ☐ Gluten Free ☐ Low Carb

Our Table Our Legacy

NAME OF DISH

RECIPE OWNER

COOK TIME

SERVINGS

INGREDIENTS

- ....
- ....
- ....
- ....
- ....
- ....
- ....
- ....
- ....
- ....
- ....

DIRECTIONS

....
....
....
....
....
....
....
....
....
....
....
....
....
....
....

notes

☐ Vegetarian   ☐ Vegan   ☐ Dairy Free   ☐ Gluten Free   ☐ Low Carb

Our Table Our Legacy

NAME OF DISH

RECIPE OWNER

COOK TIME

SERVINGS

INGREDIENTS

- ....
- ....
- ....
- ....
- ....
- ....
- ....
- ....
- ....
- ....
- ....

DIRECTIONS

notes

☐ Vegetarian   ☐ Vegan   ☐ Dairy Free   ☐ Gluten Free   ☐ Low Carb

Our Table Our Legacy

NAME OF DISH

RECIPE OWNER

COOK TIME

SERVINGS

INGREDIENTS

- ....
- ....
- ....
- ....
- ....
- ....
- ....
- ....
- ....
- ....
- ....

DIRECTIONS

notes

☐ Vegetarian   ☐ Vegan   ☐ Dairy Free   ☐ Gluten Free   ☐ Low Carb

Our Table Our Legacy

NAME OF DISH

RECIPE OWNER	COOK TIME	SERVINGS

INGREDIENTS

-
-
-
-
-
-
-
-
-
-
-

DIRECTIONS

notes

☐ Vegetarian ☐ Vegan ☐ Dairy Free ☐ Gluten Free ☐ Low Carb

Our Table Our Legacy

NAME OF DISH

RECIPE OWNER

COOK TIME

SERVINGS

INGREDIENTS

- ....
- ....
- ....
- ....
- ....
- ....
- ....
- ....
- ....
- ....
- ....

DIRECTIONS

....
....
....
....
....
....
....
....
....
....
....
....
....

notes

☐ Vegetarian ☐ Vegan ☐ Dairy Free ☐ Gluten Free ☐ Low Carb

Our Table Our Legacy

NAME OF DISH

RECIPE OWNER

COOK TIME

SERVINGS

INGREDIENTS

-
-
-
-
-
-
-
-
-
-
-

DIRECTIONS

notes

☐ Vegetarian   ☐ Vegan   ☐ Dairy Free   ☐ Gluten Free   ☐ Low Carb

DISH
PICTURE
COLLAGE

Special Ocassions

Let's *Cook*

Traditions

in our Family

Our Table Our Legacy

NAME OF DISH

RECIPE OWNER

COOK TIME

SERVINGS

INGREDIENTS

-
-
-
-
-
-
-
-
-
-
-

DIRECTIONS

notes

☐ Vegetarian ☐ Vegan ☐ Dairy Free ☐ Gluten Free ☐ Low Carb

Our Table Our Legacy

NAME OF DISH

RECIPE OWNER

COOK TIME

SERVINGS

INGREDIENTS

- ....
- ....
- ....
- ....
- ....
- ....
- ....
- ....
- ....
- ....
- ....

DIRECTIONS

notes

☐ Vegetarian   ☐ Vegan   ☐ Dairy Free   ☐ Gluten Free   ☐ Low Carb

Our Table Our Legacy

NAME OF DISH

RECIPE OWNER   COOK TIME   SERVINGS

INGREDIENTS

-
-
-
-
-
-
-
-
-
-
-

DIRECTIONS

notes

☐ Vegetarian   ☐ Vegan   ☐ Dairy Free   ☐ Gluten Free   ☐ Low Carb

Our Table Our Legacy

NAME OF DISH

RECIPE OWNER   COOK TIME   SERVINGS

INGREDIENTS

-
-
-
-
-
-
-
-
-
-
-

DIRECTIONS

notes

☐ Vegetarian   ☐ Vegan   ☐ Dairy Free   ☐ Gluten Free   ☐ Low Carb

Our Table Our Legacy

NAME OF DISH

RECIPE OWNER

COOK TIME

SERVINGS

INGREDIENTS

-
-
-
-
-
-
-
-
-
-
-

DIRECTIONS

notes

☐ Vegetarian ☐ Vegan ☐ Dairy Free ☐ Gluten Free ☐ Low Carb

Our Table Our Legacy

NAME OF DISH

RECIPE OWNER

COOK TIME

SERVINGS

INGREDIENTS

-
-
-
-
-
-
-
-
-
-
-

DIRECTIONS

notes

☐ Vegetarian   ☐ Vegan   ☐ Dairy Free   ☐ Gluten Free   ☐ Low Carb

Our Table Our Legacy

NAME OF DISH

RECIPE OWNER

COOK TIME

SERVINGS

INGREDIENTS

-
-
-
-
-
-
-
-
-
-
-

DIRECTIONS

notes

☐ Vegetarian ☐ Vegan ☐ Dairy Free ☐ Gluten Free ☐ Low Carb

Our Table Our Legacy

NAME OF DISH

RECIPE OWNER	COOK TIME	SERVINGS

INGREDIENTS

- ....
- ....
- ....
- ....
- ....
- ....
- ....
- ....
- ....
- ....
- ....

DIRECTIONS

....
....
....
....
....
....
....
....
....
....
....
....
....
....

notes

☐ Vegetarian ☐ Vegan ☐ Dairy Free ☐ Gluten Free ☐ Low Carb

Our Table Our Legacy

Our Table, Our Legacy is more than a recipe book—it is a family heirloom.

Inside these pages, you will find recipes seasoned with love, stories woven with tradition, and memories that bring warmth to every bite. Each dish reflects the laughter, faith, and togetherness that have shaped our family's journey across generations.

Whether it's a Sunday supper that brought everyone home, a holiday dessert that sweetened celebrations, or a simple dish that comforted on ordinary days, these recipes are reminders that food carries with it the legacy of family.

Pull up a chair, open these pages, and taste the stories that made us who we are. After all, every recipe tells a story—and every story keeps our legacy alive.